TRANZLATY

Language is for everyone
语言属于每个人

Beauty and the Beast

美女与野兽

Gabrielle-Suzanne Barbot de Villeneuve

English / 普通话

Copyright © 2025 Tranzlaty
All rights reserved
Published by Tranzlaty
ISBN: 978-1-83566-967-9
Original text by Gabrielle-Suzanne Barbot de Villeneuve
La Belle et la Bête
First published in French in 1740
Taken from The Blue Fairy Book (Andrew Lang)
Illustration by Walter Crane
www.tranzlaty.com

There was once a rich merchant
从前有一个富商人

this rich merchant had six children
这位富商有六个孩子

he had three sons and three daughters
他有三个儿子和三个女儿

he spared no cost for their education
他不惜一切代价来教育他们

because he was a man of sense
因为他是一个有理智的人

but he gave his children many servants
但他给了他的孩子很多仆人

his daughters were extremely pretty
他的女儿们非常漂亮

and his youngest daughter was especially pretty
他的小女儿特别漂亮

as a child her Beauty was already admired
小时候她的美貌就受到人们的赞赏

and the people called her by her Beauty
人们以她的美貌称呼她

her Beauty did not fade as she got older
她的美丽并没有随着年龄的增长而消退

so the people kept calling her by her Beauty
所以人们一直用她的美貌来称呼她

this made her sisters very jealous
这让她的姐妹们非常嫉妒

the two eldest daughters had a great deal of pride
两个大女儿非常自豪

their wealth was the source of their pride
他们的财富是他们骄傲的源泉

and they didn't hide their pride either
他们也不掩饰自己的骄傲

they did not visit other merchants' daughters
他们没有拜访其他商人的女儿

because they only meet with aristocracy
因为他们只与贵族会面
they went out every day to parties
他们每天都出去参加聚会
balls, plays, concerts, and so forth
舞会、戏剧、音乐会等
and they laughed at their youngest sister
他们嘲笑他们最小的妹妹
because she spent most of her time reading
因为她大部分时间都在读书
it was well known that they were wealthy
众所周知他们很富有
so several eminent merchants asked for their hand
于是有几位知名商人向他们求助
but they said they were not going to marry
但他们说他们不会结婚
but they were prepared to make some exceptions
但他们准备做出一些例外
"perhaps I could marry a Duke"
"也许我可以嫁给一位公爵"
"I guess I could marry an Earl"
"我想我可以嫁给一位伯爵"
Beauty very civilly thanked those that proposed to her
美女很有礼貌地感谢那些向她求婚的人
she told them she was still too young to marry
她告诉他们她还太年轻,不适合结婚
she wanted to stay a few more years with her father
她想和父亲多呆几年
All at once the merchant lost his fortune
商人一下子失去了他的财富
he lost everything apart from a small country house
除了一栋乡间小别墅外,他失去了一切
and he told his children with tears in his eyes:
他热泪盈眶地告诉他的孩子们:

"we must go to the countryside"
"我们必须去乡下"
"and we must work for our living"
"我们必须工作才能生存"
the two eldest daughters didn't want to leave the town
两个大女儿不想离开小镇
they had several lovers in the city
他们在城里有几个情人
and they were sure one of their lovers would marry them
她们确信她们的情人中一定会有一个娶她们为妻
they thought their lovers would marry them even with no fortune
她们认为即使自己没有财产，爱人也会娶她们为妻
but the good ladies were mistaken
但这些好心的女士们错了
their lovers abandoned them very quickly
他们的爱人很快就抛弃了他们
because they had no fortunes any more
因为他们再也没有财富了
this showed they were not actually well liked
这表明他们实际上并不受欢迎
everybody said they do not deserve to be pitied
大家都说他们不值得同情
"we are glad to see their pride humbled"
"我们很高兴看到他们的骄傲被贬低了"
"let them be proud of milking cows"
"让他们为挤牛奶而感到自豪"
but they were concerned for Beauty
但他们关心的是美丽
she was such a sweet creature
她真是一个可爱的人
she spoke so kindly to poor people
她对穷人说话很亲切
and she was of such an innocent nature

她天性如此纯真
Several gentlemen would have married her
很多绅士都会娶她
they would have married her even though she was poor
尽管她很穷,他们也会娶她
but she told them she couldn't marry them
但她告诉他们她不能嫁给他们
because she would not leave her father
因为她不愿离开她的父亲
she was determined to go with him to the countryside
她决心和他一起去乡下
so that she could comfort and help him
以便她能安慰和帮助他
Poor Beauty was very grieved at first
可怜的美女一开始很伤心
she was grieved by the loss of her fortune
她因失去财产而悲痛
"but crying won't change my fortunes"
"但哭泣不会改变我的命运"
"I must try to make myself happy without wealth"
"即使没有财富,我也必须努力让自己快乐"
they came to their country house
他们来到了乡间别墅
and the merchant and his three sons applied themselves to husbandry
商人和他的三个儿子致力于农业
Beauty rose at four in the morning
美丽在凌晨四点升起
and she hurried to clean the house
她赶紧打扫房子
and she made sure dinner was ready
她确保晚餐准备好了
in the beginning she found her new life very difficult
一开始她发现新生活非常困难

because she had not been used to such work
因为她还不习惯这样的工作
but in less than two months she grew stronger
但不到两个月她就变得更强壮了
and she was healthier than ever before
她比以前更健康了
after she had done her work she read
做完作业后她读了
she played on the harpsichord
她弹奏大键琴
or she sung whilst she spun silk
或者她一边唱歌一边纺丝
on the contrary, her two sisters did not know how to spend their time
相反,她的两个姐姐不知道如何打发时间
they got up at ten and did nothing but laze about all day
他们十点起床,整天无所事事,只是懒散地度过
they lamented the loss of their fine clothes
他们为失去漂亮的衣服而感到悲痛
and they complained about losing their acquaintances
他们抱怨失去熟人
"Have a look at our youngest sister," they said to each other
他们互相说道:"看看我们最小的妹妹。"
"what a poor and stupid creature she is"
"她真是一个可怜又愚蠢的人"
"it is mean to be content with so little"
"满足于如此之少是卑鄙的"
the kind merchant was of quite a different opinion
这位好心的商人却持不同意见
he knew very well that Beauty outshone her sisters
他很清楚,她的美丽胜过她的姐妹们
she outshone them in character as well as mind
她的性格和思想都比他们出色
he admired her humility and her hard work

他钦佩她的谦逊和勤奋
but most of all he admired her patience
但他最钦佩的是她的耐心
her sisters left her all the work to do
她的姐姐们把所有的工作都留给了她
and they insulted her every moment
他们时刻侮辱她
The family had lived like this for about a year
这家人这样生活了大约一年
then the merchant got a letter from an accountant
然后商人收到一封会计师的信
he had an investment in a ship
他投资了一艘船
and the ship had safely arrived
船已安全抵达
this news turned the heads of the two eldest daughters
这消息让两个大女儿大吃一惊
they immediately had hopes of returning to town
他们立刻有了返回城镇的希望
because they were quite weary of country life
因为他们已经厌倦了乡村生活
they went to their father as he was leaving
父亲正要离开时，他们去了他那里
they begged him to buy them new clothes
他们求他给他们买新衣服
dresses, ribbons, and all sorts of little things
裙子、丝带和各种小东西
but Beauty asked for nothing
但美丽却不求回报
because she thought the money wasn't going to be enough
因为她认为钱不够
there wouldn't be enough to buy everything her sisters wanted
没有足够的钱来购买她姐妹们想要的所有东西

"What would you like, Beauty?" asked her father
"美女,你想要什么?"父亲问。

"thank you, father, for the goodness to think of me," she said
"谢谢爸爸,谢谢你对我的关心。"她说

"father, be so kind as to bring me a rose"
"爸爸,请送我一朵玫瑰花吧"

"because no roses grow here in the garden"
"因为花园里没有玫瑰"

"and roses are a kind of rarity"
"玫瑰是一种珍品"

Beauty didn't really care for roses
美女并不在乎玫瑰

she only asked for something not to condemn her sisters
她只是要求不要谴责她的姐妹们

but her sisters thought she asked for roses for other reasons
但她的姐妹们认为她要玫瑰花是出于其他原因

"she did it just to look particular"
"她这么做只是为了显得特别"

The kind man went on his journey
这位善良的男子继续他的旅程

but when he arrived they argued about the merchandise
但当他到达时,他们就商品发生争执

and after a lot of trouble he came back as poor as before
经过一番折腾,他又回来了,和以前一样穷困潦倒

he was within a couple of hours of his own house
他离家只有几个小时的车程

and he already imagined the joy of seeing his children
他已经想象到看到孩子们的喜悦

but when going through forest he got lost
但当他穿过森林时他迷路了

it rained and snowed terribly
雨雪交加

the wind was so strong it threw him off his horse
风太大了,把他从马上吹下来

and night was coming quickly
夜幕很快降临

he began to think that he might starve
他开始担心自己可能会饿死

and he thought that he might freeze to death
他觉得自己可能会被冻死

and he thought wolves may eat him
他认为狼可能会吃掉他

the wolves that he heard howling all round him
他听到周围狼嚎叫

but all of a sudden he saw a light
但突然间他看到了一道光

he saw the light at a distance through the trees
他透过树木看见远处的光

when he got closer he saw the light was a palace
当他走近时，他发现光是一座宫殿

the palace was illuminated from top to bottom
宫殿从上到下都灯火通明

the merchant thanked God for his luck
商人感谢上帝给了他好运

and he hurried to the palace
他赶紧去了宫殿

but he was surprised to see no people in the palace
但他惊讶地发现宫殿里没有人

the court yard was completely empty
院子里空无一人

and there was no sign of life anywhere
任何地方都没有生命迹象

his horse followed him into the palace
他的马跟着他进了宫殿

and then his horse found large stable
然后他的马找到了一个大马厩

the poor animal was almost famished
这只可怜的动物几乎饿死了

so his horse went in to find hay and oats
于是他的马就去找干草和燕麦
fortunately he found plenty to eat
幸运的是他找到了很多吃的
and the merchant tied his horse up to the manger
商人把马拴在马槽边
walking towards the house he saw no one
走向房子时他没有看到任何人
but in a large hall he found a good fire
但在大厅里他发现了一堆好火
and he found a table set for one
他找到一张单人桌
he was wet from the rain and snow
他被雨雪淋湿了
so he went near the fire to dry himself
于是他走到火边烤干身体
"I hope the master of the house will excuse me"
"希望主人能原谅我"
"I suppose it won't take long for someone to appear"
"我想很快就会有人出现了。"
He waited a considerable time
他等了相当长一段时间
he waited until it struck eleven, and still nobody came
他一直等到十一点，还是没人来
at last he was so hungry that he could wait no longer
最后他饿得再也等不及了
he took some chicken and ate it in two mouthfuls
他拿了一些鸡肉，两口就吃了下去
he was trembling while eating the food
他吃东西的时候浑身发抖
after this he drank a few glasses of wine
之后他喝了几杯酒
growing more courageous he went out of the hall
他鼓起勇气走出了大厅

and he crossed through several grand halls
他穿过了几个大厅

he walked through the palace until he came into a chamber
他穿过宫殿,来到一个房间

a chamber which had an exceeding good bed in it
房间里有一张非常舒适的床

he was very much fatigued from his ordeal
他因这场磨难而疲惫不堪

and the time was already past midnight
当时已经过了午夜

so he decided it was best to shut the door
所以他决定最好关上门

and he concluded he should go to bed
他决定去睡觉了

It was ten in the morning when the merchant woke up
商人醒来时是早上十点

just as he was going to rise he saw something
正当他要起身时,他看见了一些东西

he was astonished to see a clean set of clothes
他惊讶地看到一套干净的衣服

in the place where he had left his dirty clothes
在他放脏衣服的地方

"certainly this palace belongs to some kind fairy"
"这座宫殿肯定是属于某位善良的仙女的"

"a fairy who has seen and pitied me"
"一位仙女看见了我并可怜我"

he looked through a window
他透过窗户往里看

but instead of snow he saw the most delightful garden
但他看到的不是雪,而是最美丽的花园

and in the garden were the most beautiful roses
花园里有最美丽的玫瑰

he then returned to the great hall
然后他回到了大厅

the hall where he had had soup the night before
他前一天晚上喝汤的大厅
and he found some chocolate on a little table
他在小桌子上发现了一些巧克力
"Thank you, good Madam Fairy," he said aloud
"谢谢您，好仙女，"他大声说道。
"thank you for being so caring"
"谢谢你这么关心"
"I am extremely obliged to you for all your favours"
"我非常感谢你的帮助"
the kind man drank his chocolate
这位好心人喝了他的巧克力
and then he went to look for his horse
然后他去找他的马
but in the garden he remembered Beauty's request
但在花园里他想起了美女的请求
and he cut off a branch of roses
他砍下一枝玫瑰
immediately he heard a great noise
他立刻听到了巨大的响声
and he saw a terribly frightful Beast
他看到了一只非常可怕的野兽
he was so scared that he was ready to faint
他吓得快晕过去了
"You are very ungrateful," said the Beast to him
"你太不知感恩了，"野兽对他说
and the Beast spoke in a terrible voice
野兽用可怕的声音说话
"I have saved your life by allowing you into my castle"
"我让你进入我的城堡，救了你的命"
"and for this you steal my roses in return?"
"而你就为了这个偷走了我的玫瑰花？"
"The roses which I value beyond anything"
"我最珍视的玫瑰"

"but you shall die for what you've done"
"但你会因你所做的事而死"

"I give you but a quarter of an hour to prepare yourself"
"我只给你一刻钟的时间准备"

"get yourself ready for death and say your prayers"
"做好死亡的准备并祈祷"

the merchant fell on his knees
商人跪倒在地

and he lifted up both his hands
他举起双手

"My lord, I beseech you to forgive me"
"大人,请您原谅我"

"I had no intention of offending you"
"我无意冒犯你"

"I gathered a rose for one of my daughters"
"我为我的一个女儿采了一朵玫瑰"

"she asked me to bring her a rose"
"她让我给她带一朵玫瑰"

"I am not your lord, but I am a Beast," replied the monster
"我不是你的主人,我是一头野兽。" 怪物回答道

"I don't love compliments"
"我不喜欢赞美"

"I like people who speak as they think"
"我喜欢说话直率的人"

"do not imagine I can be moved by flattery"
"别以为我能被奉承打动"

"But you say you have got daughters"
"但你说你有女儿"

"I will forgive you on one condition"
"我原谅你,但有一个条件"

"one of your daughters must come to my palace willingly"
"你的一个女儿必须自愿来到我的宫殿"

"and she must suffer for you"
"她必须为你受苦"

"Let me have your word"
"请允许我向你保证"
"and then you can go about your business"
"然后你就可以去做你的事了"
"Promise me this:"
"答应我："
"if your daughter refuses to die for you, you must return within three months"
"如果你的女儿不肯为你而死,你必须在三个月内回来"
the merchant had no intentions to sacrifice his daughters
商人无意牺牲自己的女儿
but, since he was given time, he wanted to see his daughters once more
但既然有时间,他想再见见女儿们
so he promised he would return
所以他答应他会回来
and the Beast told him he might set out when he pleased
野兽告诉他,他可以随时出发
and the Beast told him one more thing
野兽又告诉他一件事
"you shall not depart empty handed"
"你不会空手而归"
"go back to the room where you lay"
"回到你躺着的房间去"
"you will see a great empty treasure chest"
"你会看到一个巨大的空宝箱"
"fill the treasure chest with whatever you like best"
"用你最喜欢的东西填满宝箱"
"and I will send the treasure chest to your home"
"我会把宝箱送到你家"
and at the same time the Beast withdrew
与此同时,野兽撤退了
"Well," said the good man to himself

"好吧,"好人自言自语道。

"if I must die, I shall at least leave something to my children"
"如果我必须死,我至少会给我的孩子留下一些东西
"

so he returned to the bedchamber
于是他回到卧室
and he found a great many pieces of gold
他发现了许多金币
he filled the treasure chest the Beast had mentioned
他装满了野兽提到的宝箱
and he took his horse out of the stable
他把马从马厩里牵出来
the joy he felt when entering the palace was now equal to the grief he felt leaving it
他进入宫殿时的喜悦现在等于离开宫殿时的悲伤
the horse took one of the roads of the forest
马走上了森林的一条路
and in a few hours the good man was home
几个小时后,这位好心人就回家了
his children came to him
他的孩子们来到他身边
but instead of receiving their embraces with pleasure, he looked at them
但他并没有高兴地接受他们的拥抱,而是看着他们
he held up the branch he had in his hands
他举起手中的树枝
and then he burst into tears
然后他泪流满面
"Beauty," he said, "please take these roses"
"美女,"他说,"请收下这些玫瑰"
"you can't know how costly these roses have been"
"你不知道这些玫瑰有多贵"
"these roses have cost your father his life"

"这些玫瑰害死了你父亲"
and then he told of his fatal adventure
然后他讲述了他的致命冒险
immediately the two eldest sisters cried out
两个姐姐立刻叫了起来
and they said many mean things to their beautiful sister
他们对他们美丽的妹妹说了很多刻薄的话
but Beauty did not cry at all
但美女一点都没哭
"Look at the pride of that little wretch," said they
"看看这个小家伙的骄傲，"他们说
"she did not ask for fine clothes"
"她并不要求穿华丽的衣服"
"she should have done what we did"
"她应该像我们一样"
"she wanted to distinguish herself"
"她想让自己与众不同"
"so now she will be the death of our father"
"所以现在她将成为我们父亲的死敌"
"and yet she does not shed a tear"
"但她却没有流一滴泪"
"Why should I cry?" answered Beauty
美女回答："我为什么要哭？"
"crying would be very needless"
"哭泣是没有必要的"
"my father will not suffer for me"
"我父亲不会为我受苦"
"the monster will accept of one of his daughters"
"怪物会接受他的一个女儿"
"I will offer myself up to all his fury"
"我将献出自己，承受他所有的愤怒"
"I am very happy, because my death will save my father's life"
"我很高兴，因为我的死将挽救我父亲的生命"

"my death will be a proof of my love"
"我的死将证明我的爱"

"No, sister," said her three brothers
三个哥哥都说:"不,姐姐。"

"that shall not be"
"那不可能"

"we will go find the monster"
"我们去找怪物"

"and either we will kill him..."
"要么我们就杀了他……"

"... or we will perish in the attempt"
"...否则我们将在尝试中灭亡"

"Do not imagine any such thing, my sons," said the merchant
"别想这些,我的孩子,"商人说。

"the Beast's power is so great that I have no hope you could overcome him"
"这头野兽的力量太强大了,我不认为你能战胜他"

"I am charmed with Beauty's kind and generous offer"
"我被美女的善良和慷慨所吸引"

"but I cannot accept to her generosity"
"但我不能接受她的慷慨"

"I am old, and I don't have long to live"
"我老了,活不了多久了"

"so I can only loose a few years"
"所以我只能损失几年"

"time which I regret for you, my dear children"
"我为你们感到遗憾的时刻,我亲爱的孩子们"

"But father," said Beauty
美女说:"可是爸爸。"

"you shall not go to the palace without me"
"没有我陪同,你不能去宫殿"

"you cannot stop me from following you"
"你不能阻止我跟随你"

nothing could convince Beauty otherwise

没有什么能够改变美丽
she insisted on going to the fine palace
她坚持要去那座美丽的宫殿
and her sisters were delighted at her insistence
她的姐妹们对她的坚持感到高兴
The merchant was worried at the thought of losing his daughter
商人担心会失去女儿
he was so worried that he had forgotten about the chest full of gold
他太担心了，忘记了装满金子的箱子
at night he retired to rest, and he shut his chamber door
晚上他休息，关上房门。
then, to his great astonishment, he found the treasure by his bedside
然后，令他大为惊讶的是，他在床边发现了宝藏
he was determined not to tell his children
他决心不告诉他的孩子
if they knew, they would have wanted to return to town
如果他们知道的话，他们就会想回到城里
and he was resolved not to leave the countryside
他决心不离开乡村
but he trusted Beauty with the secret
但他相信美丽能带来秘密
she informed him that two gentlemen had came
她告诉他有两位先生来了
and they made proposals to her sisters
他们向她的姐妹们求婚
she begged her father to consent to their marriage
她恳求父亲同意他们的婚事
and she asked him to give them some of his fortune
她要求他给他们一些财产
she had already forgiven them
她已经原谅他们了

the wicked creatures rubbed their eyes with onions
邪恶的生物用洋葱揉眼睛
to force some tears when they parted with their sister
在与姐姐告别时强颜欢笑
but her brothers really were concerned
但她的兄弟们确实很担心
Beauty was the only one who did not shed any tears
美女是唯一一个没有流泪的人
she did not want to increase their uneasiness
她不想增加他们的不安
the horse took the direct road to the palace
马直接走路去宫殿
and towards evening they saw the illuminated palace
傍晚时分，他们看到了灯火通明的宫殿
the horse took himself into the stable again
马又回到了马厩
and the good man and his daughter went into the great hall
好心人和他的女儿走进大厅
here they found a table splendidly served up
他们在这里找到了一张精心准备的桌子
the merchant had no appetite to eat
商人没有胃口吃饭
but Beauty endeavoured to appear cheerful
但美丽却努力表现出快乐
she sat down at the table and helped her father
她坐在桌边，帮助父亲
but she also thought to herself:
但她心里也在想：
"Beast surely wants to fatten me before he eats me"
"野兽肯定想先把我养肥再吃掉我"
"that is why he provides such plentiful entertainment"
"这就是为什么他提供如此丰富的娱乐"
after they had eaten they heard a great noise
吃完饭后，他们听到了巨大的响声

and the merchant bid his unfortunate child farewell, with tears in his eyes
商人含着泪水向不幸的孩子告别。
because he knew the Beast was coming
因为他知道野兽即将来临
Beauty was terrified at his horrid form
美女被他可怕的外表吓坏了
but she took courage as well as she could
但她鼓起勇气
and the monster asked her if she came willingly
怪物问她是否愿意来
"yes, I have come willingly," she said trembling
"是的，我自愿来的，"她颤抖着说
the Beast responded, "You are very good"
野兽回答说："你很厉害。"
"and I am greatly obliged to you; honest man"
"我非常感谢你，你是一个诚实的人。"
"go your ways tomorrow morning"
"明天早上走吧"
"but never think of coming here again"
"但永远不要再想来这里"
"Farewell Beauty, farewell Beast," he answered
"再见，美女，再见，野兽。"他回答道
and immediately the monster withdrew
怪物立刻撤退了
"Oh, daughter," said the merchant
"哦，女儿，"商人说。
and he embraced his daughter once more
他再次拥抱了女儿
"I am almost frightened to death"
"我快被吓死了"
"believe me, you had better go back"
"相信我，你最好回去"
"let me stay here, instead of you"

"让我代替你留在这里"
"No, father," said Beauty, in a resolute tone
美女坚决地说:"不,爸爸。"
"you shall set out tomorrow morning"
"你明天早上就出发"
"leave me to the care and protection of providence"
"让我接受上帝的照顾和保护"
nonetheless they went to bed
尽管如此他们还是去睡觉了
they thought they would not close their eyes all night
他们以为自己一整晚都不会合眼
but just as they lay down they slept
但当他们躺下时他们就睡着了
Beauty dreamed a fine lady came and said to her:
美女梦见一位美丽的女士来到她面前,对她说:
"I am content, Beauty, with your good will"
"我很满足,美女,有你的善意"
"this good action of yours shall not go unrewarded"
"你的善举不会得不到回报"
Beauty waked and told her father her dream
美女醒来后告诉父亲她的梦
the dream helped to comfort him a little
这个梦让他稍感安慰
but he could not help crying bitterly as he was leaving
但他临走时还是忍不住痛哭流涕
as soon as he was gone, Beauty sat down in the great hall and cried too
他一走,美女就坐在大厅里哭了
but she resolved not to be uneasy
但她决心不感到不安
she decided to be strong for the little time she had left to live
她决定在生命所剩无几的时间里保持坚强
because she firmly believed the Beast would eat her
因为她坚信野兽会吃掉她

however, she thought she might as well explore the palace
然而,她认为她最好去探索宫殿
and she wanted to view the fine castle
她想看看美丽的城堡
a castle which she could not help admiring
一座令她情不自禁赞叹的城堡
it was a delightfully pleasant palace
这是一座令人愉悦的宫殿
and she was extremely surprised at seeing a door
她非常惊讶地看到一扇门
and over the door was written that it was her room
门上写着这是她的房间
she opened the door hastily
她急忙打开了门
and she was quite dazzled with the magnificence of the room
她被房间的华丽所震撼
what chiefly took up her attention was a large library
最吸引她注意的是一座大图书馆
a harpsichord and several music books
一架大键琴和几本乐谱
"Well," said she to herself
"好吧," 她自言自语道。
"I see the Beast will not let my time hang heavy"
"我知道野兽不会让我的时间过得那么沉重"
then she reflected to herself about her situation
然后她反思了自己的处境
"If I was meant to stay a day all this would not be here"
"如果我只留下一天,这一切都不会发生"
this consideration inspired her with fresh courage
这种考虑激发了她新的勇气
and she took a book from her new library
她从新图书馆里拿了一本书
and she read these words in golden letters:

她读到了金色大字：
"Welcome Beauty, banish fear"
"欢迎美丽，驱逐恐惧"
"You are queen and mistress here"
"你是这里的女王和女主人"
"Speak your wishes, speak your will"
"说出你的愿望，说出你的意愿"
"Swift obedience meets your wishes here"
"快速服从在这里满足了你的愿望"
"Alas," said she, with a sigh
"唉，"她叹了一口气说。
"Most of all I wish to see my poor father"
"我最想见到的是我可怜的父亲"
"and I would like to know what he is doing"
"我想知道他在做什么"
As soon as she had said this she noticed the mirror
她刚说完这句话，就注意到了镜子
to her great amazement she saw her own home in the mirror
令她惊讶的是，她在镜子里看到了自己的家
her father arrived emotionally exhausted
她父亲回来时已经精疲力尽
her sisters went to meet him
她的姐妹们去见他
despite their attempts to appear sorrowful, their joy was visible
尽管他们试图表现出悲伤，但他们的喜悦是显而易见的
a moment later everything disappeared
片刻之后一切都消失了
and Beauty's apprehensions disappeared too
美丽的忧虑也消失了
for she knew she could trust the Beast
因为她知道她可以相信野兽
At noon she found dinner ready

中午时她发现晚饭已经做好了
she sat herself down at the table
她坐在桌边
and she was entertained with a concert of music
她欣赏了一场音乐会
although she couldn't see anybody
尽管她没看见任何人
at night she sat down for supper again
晚上她又坐下来吃晚饭
this time she heard the noise the Beast made
这次她听到了野兽发出的声音
and she could not help being terrified
她不禁感到害怕
"Beauty," said the monster
"美女,"怪物说
"do you allow me to eat with you?"
"你允许我跟你一起吃饭吗?"
"do as you please," Beauty answered trembling
"随你便吧。"美女颤抖着回答
"No," replied the Beast
"不,"野兽回答道
"you alone are mistress here"
"你才是这里的主人"
"you can send me away if I'm troublesome"
"如果我惹麻烦的话你可以把我打发走"
"send me away and I will immediately withdraw"
"送我走,我马上撤退"
"But, tell me; do you not think I am very ugly?"
"但是,告诉我;你不觉得我很丑吗?"
"That is true," said Beauty
美女道:"那倒是。"
"I cannot tell a lie"
"我不能撒谎"
"but I believe you are very good natured"

"但我相信你心地很好"
"I am indeed," said the monster
"我确实是,"怪物说。
"But apart from my ugliness, I also have no sense"
"但我除了丑之外,也没有智慧。"
"I know very well that I am a silly creature"
"我很清楚我是一个愚蠢的生物"
"It is no sign of folly to think so," replied Beauty
"这样想并不愚蠢,"美女回答道
"Eat then, Beauty," said the monster
"那就吃吧,美女。"怪物说
"try to amuse yourself in your palace"
"在宫殿里尽情玩乐吧"
"everything here is yours"
"这里的一切都是你的"
"and I would be very uneasy if you were not happy"
"如果你不开心,我会很不安"
"You are very obliging," answered Beauty
"你真好心,"美女回答道
"I admit I am pleased with your kindness"
"我承认我对你的善意感到高兴"
"and when I consider your kindness, I hardly notice your deformities"
"当我想到你的善良时,我几乎没注意到你的缺陷"
"Yes, yes," said the Beast, "my heart is good
"是的,是的,"野兽说,"我的心是善良的
"but although I am good, I am still a monster"
"尽管我很善良,但我依然是个怪物"
"There are many men that deserve that name more than you"
"有很多男人比你更配得上这个名字"
"and I prefer you just as you are"
"我更喜欢你本来的样子"
"and I prefer you more than those who hide an ungrateful heart"

"我更喜欢你,而不是那些心怀不轨的人"
"if only I had some sense," replied the Beast
"要是我还有点理智就好了。"野兽回答道
"if I had sense I would make a fine compliment to thank you"
"如果我有理智,我会用赞美来感谢你"
"but I am so dull"
"但我很无聊"
"I can only say I am greatly obliged to you"
"我只能说我非常感谢你"
Beauty ate a hearty supper
美女吃了一顿丰盛的晚餐
and she had almost conquered her dread of the monster
她几乎已经克服了对怪物的恐惧
but she wanted to faint when the Beast asked her the next question
但当野兽问她下一个问题时,她想晕过去
"Beauty, will you be my wife?"
"美女,你愿意做我的老婆吗?"
she took some time before she could answer
她过了一会儿才回答
because she was afraid of making him angry
因为她害怕惹他生气
at last, however, she said "no, Beast"
但最后她说"不,野兽"
immediately the poor monster hissed very frightfully
这可怜的怪物立刻发出可怕的嘶嘶声
and the whole palace echoed
整个宫殿回响着
but Beauty soon recovered from her fright
但美女很快就从恐惧中恢复过来
because Beast spoke again in a mournful voice
因为野兽又用悲伤的声音说话了
"then farewell, Beauty"

"那么再见了，美女"

and he only turned back now and then
他只是偶尔回头

to look at her as he went out
在他出去的时候看着她

now Beauty was alone again
现在美丽又孤单了

she felt a great deal of compassion
她感到十分同情

"Alas, it is a thousand pities"
"唉，真是可惜啊"

"anything so good natured should not be so ugly"
"如此善良的事物不应该如此丑陋"

Beauty spent three months very contentedly in the palace
美女在宫中过得很满足

every evening the Beast paid her a visit
每天晚上，野兽都会来拜访她

and they talked during supper
他们在晚餐时聊天

they talked with common sense
他们说话有常识

but they didn't talk with what people call wittiness
但他们说话并不像人们所说的那样机智

Beauty always discovered some valuable character in the Beast
美女总能发现野兽身上的某些宝贵品质

and she had gotten used to his deformity
她已经习惯了他的畸形

she didn't dread the time of his visit anymore
她不再害怕他的到来

now she often looked at her watch
现在她经常看手表

and she couldn't wait for it to be nine o'clock
她迫不及待地等着九点

because the Beast never missed coming at that hour
因为野兽从不会错过那个时刻
there was only one thing that concerned Beauty
只有一件事与美丽有关
every night before she went to bed the Beast asked her the same question
每天晚上睡觉前，野兽都会问她同样的问题
the monster asked her if she would be his wife
怪物问她是否愿意成为他的妻子
one day she said to him, "Beast, you make me very uneasy"
有一天她对他说："野兽，你让我很不安"
"I wish I could consent to marry you"
"我希望我能同意嫁给你"
"but I am too sincere to make you believe I would marry you"
"但我太真诚了，让你相信我会娶你"
"our marriage will never happen"
"我们的婚姻永远不会实现"
"I shall always see you as a friend"
"我会永远把你视为朋友"
"please try to be satisfied with this"
"请尽量对此感到满意"
"I must be satisfied with this," said the Beast
"我必须对此感到满意，"野兽说
"I know my own misfortune"
"我知道我自己的不幸"
"but I love you with the tenderest affection"
"但我以最温柔的感情爱你"
"However, I ought to consider myself as happy"
"但我应该认为自己很幸福"
"and I should be happy that you will stay here"
"我很高兴你能留在这里"
"promise me never to leave me"
"答应我永远不要离开我"

Beauty blushed at these words
美女听了这些话脸红了

one day Beauty was looking in her mirror
有一天,美女看着镜子里的自己

her father had worried himself sick for her
她的父亲为她操心

she longed to see him again more than ever
她比以往任何时候都渴望再次见到他

"I could promise never to leave you entirely"
"我可以保证永远不会离开你"

"but I have so great a desire to see my father"
"但我非常想见到我的父亲"

"I would be impossibly upset if you say no"
"如果你拒绝我,我会非常难过"

"I had rather die myself," said the monster
"我宁愿自己去死。"怪物说

"I would rather die than make you feel uneasiness"
"我宁愿死,也不愿让你感到不安"

"I will send you to your father"
"我会送你去见你父亲"

"you shall remain with him"
"你应该和他在一起"

"and this unfortunate Beast will die with grief instead"
"而这只不幸的野兽将会悲伤地死去"

"No," said Beauty, weeping
美女哭着说:"不。"

"I love you too much to be the cause of your death"
"我太爱你了,所以不能成为你的死因"

"I give you my promise to return in a week"
"我保证一周后回来"

"You have shown me that my sisters are married"
"你告诉我我的姐姐们都结婚了"

"and my brothers have gone to the army"
"我的兄弟们都去参军了"

"let me stay a week with my father, as he is alone"
"让我和我父亲待一个星期,因为他一个人。"

"You shall be there tomorrow morning," said the Beast
"明天早上你就得去那里。"野兽说

"but remember your promise"
"但要记住你的承诺"

"You need only lay your ring on a table before you go to bed"
"你只需要在睡觉前把戒指放在桌子上"

"and then you will be brought back before the morning"
"然后你会在早晨之前被带回来"

"Farewell dear Beauty," sighed the Beast
"再见了,亲爱的美人。"野兽叹息道

Beauty went to bed very sad that night
美女那天晚上很伤心地睡觉了

because she didn't want to see Beast so worried
因为她不想看到野兽如此担心

the next morning she found herself at her father's home
第二天早上,她来到了父亲的家

she rung a little bell by her bedside
她按响了床边的一个小铃铛

and the maid gave a loud shriek
女仆尖叫起来

and her father ran upstairs
她爸爸跑上楼

he thought he was going to die with joy
他以为自己会高兴地死去

he held her in his arms for quarter of an hour
他把她抱在怀里足足一刻钟

eventually the first greetings were over
终于,第一声问候结束了

Beauty began to think of getting out of bed
美女开始想起床

but she realized she had brought no clothes

但她意识到自己没带衣服
but the maid told her she had found a box
但女仆告诉她,她发现了一个盒子
the large trunk was full of gowns and dresses
大箱子里装满了礼服和连衣裙
each gown was covered with gold and diamonds
每件礼服都镶满了黄金和钻石
Beauty thanked Beast for his kind care
美女感谢野兽的善意照顾
and she took one of the plainest of the dresses
她选了一件最朴素的衣服
she intended to give the other dresses to her sisters
她打算把其他的衣服送给她的姐妹们
but at that thought the chest of clothes disappeared
但一想到这里,衣服箱就消失了
Beast had insisted the clothes were for her only
野兽坚称这些衣服只适合她
her father told her that this was the case
她父亲告诉她情况就是这样
and immediately the trunk of clothes came back again
衣服箱子立刻又回来了
Beauty dressed herself with her new clothes
美女穿上新衣服
and in the meantime maids went to find her sisters
与此同时,女仆们去找她的姐妹们
both her sister were with their husbands
她的两个姐姐和她们的丈夫在一起
but both her sisters were very unhappy
但她的两个姐妹都很不开心
her eldest sister had married a very handsome gentleman
她大姐嫁给了一位非常英俊的绅士
but he was so fond of himself that he neglected his wife
但他太自私了,忽视了妻子
her second sister had married a witty man

她的二姐嫁给了一个机智的男人
but he used his wittiness to torment people
但他用他的机智来折磨人
and he tormented his wife most of all
他最折磨的是他的妻子
Beauty's sisters saw her dressed like a princess
美女的姐妹们看到她穿得像个公主
and they were sickened with envy
他们嫉妒得要死
now she was more beautiful than ever
现在她比以前更美丽了
her affectionate behaviour could not stifle their jealousy
她的亲热行为无法抑制他们的嫉妒
she told them how happy she was with the Beast
她告诉他们她和这头野兽在一起有多开心
and their jealousy was ready to burst
他们的嫉妒心即将爆发
They went down into the garden to cry about their misfortune
他们走进花园，哭诉他们的不幸遭遇
"In what way is this little creature better than us?"
"这个小动物在哪些方面比我们优秀呢？"
"Why should she be so much happier?"
"为什么她应该这么高兴？"
"Sister," said the older sister
"姐姐，"姐姐说
"a thought just struck my mind"
"我突然想到了一个主意"
"let us try to keep her here for more than a week"
"我们试着让她在这里待一个多星期"
"perhaps this will enrage the silly monster"
"也许这会激怒这个愚蠢的怪物"
"because she would have broken her word"
"因为她会食言"

"and then he might devour her"
"然后他可能会吞噬她"

"that's a great idea," answered the other sister
"这是个好主意，"另一个姐妹回答道

"we must show her as much kindness as possible"
"我们必须尽可能地向她表示善意"

the sisters made this their resolution
姐妹们下定决心

and they behaved very affectionately to their sister
他们对待姐妹非常亲热

poor Beauty wept for joy from all their kindness
可怜的美人因他们的善意而喜极而泣

when the week was expired, they cried and tore their hair
一周结束后，他们哭了，扯着头发

they seemed so sorry to part with her
他们似乎很舍不得和她分开

and Beauty promised to stay a week longer
美女答应再呆一周

In the meantime, Beauty could not help reflecting on herself
与此同时，美女不禁反思自己

she worried what she was doing to poor Beast
她担心自己对可怜的动物做了什么

she know that she sincerely loved him
她知道她真心爱他

and she really longed to see him again
她真的很想再次见到他

the tenth night she spent at her father's too
第十天晚上，她在父亲家也

she dreamed she was in the palace garden
她梦见自己在宫殿花园里

and she dreamt she saw the Beast extended on the grass
她梦见那头野兽躺在草地上

he seemed to reproach her in a dying voice
他似乎在用垂死的声音责备她

and he accused her of ingratitude
他指责她忘恩负义

Beauty woke up from her sleep
美女从睡梦中醒来

and she burst into tears
她泪流满面

"Am I not very wicked?"
"我是不是太坏了？"

"Was it not cruel of me to act so unkindly to the Beast?"
"我对这头野兽如此不友善，难道不是很残忍吗？"

"Beast did everything to please me"
"野兽为取悦我做了一切"

"Is it his fault that he is so ugly?"
"他这么丑是他的错吗？"

"Is it his fault that he has so little wit?"
"他这么缺乏智慧，这是他的错吗？"

"He is kind and good, and that is sufficient"
"他很善良，这就足够了"

"Why did I refuse to marry him?"
"我为什么拒绝嫁给他？"

"I should be happy with the monster"
"我应该对怪物感到高兴"

"look at the husbands of my sisters"
"看看我姐姐们的丈夫"

"neither wittiness, nor a being handsome makes them good"
"机智和英俊都不能使他们变得优秀"

"neither of their husbands makes them happy"
"她们的丈夫都没有让她们幸福"

"but virtue, sweetness of temper, and patience"
"而是美德、温和的脾气和耐心"

"these things make a woman happy"
"这些东西让女人感到幸福"

"and the Beast has all these valuable qualities"
"而野兽拥有所有这些宝贵的品质"

"it is true; I do not feel the tenderness of affection for him"
"是的，我对他没有一丝感情。"

"but I find I have the highest gratitude for him"
"但我对他怀有最崇高的感激之情"

"and I have the highest esteem of him"
"我非常尊重他"

"and he is my best friend"
"他是我最好的朋友"

"I will not make him miserable"
"我不会让他痛苦"

"If were I to be so ungrateful I would never forgive myself"
"如果我如此忘恩负义，我永远不会原谅自己"

Beauty put her ring on the table
美女把戒指放在桌子上

and she went to bed again
然后她又去睡觉了

scarce was she in bed before she fell asleep
她刚上床就睡着了

she woke up again the next morning
第二天早上她又醒了

and she was overjoyed to find herself in the Beast's palace
她欣喜若狂地发现自己身处野兽的宫殿

she put on one of her nicest dress to please him
她穿上了她最漂亮的衣服来取悦他

and she patiently waited for evening
她耐心地等待着夜晚

at last the wished-for hour came
到了盼望的时刻

the clock struck nine, yet no Beast appeared
时钟敲响九点，却没有野兽出现

Beauty then feared she had been the cause of his death
美女当时担心她是导致他死亡的原因

she ran crying all around the palace
她哭着跑遍了宫殿

after having sought for him everywhere, she remembered her dream
在到处寻找他之后,她想起了自己的梦
and she ran to the canal in the garden
她跑到花园里的运河
there she found poor Beast stretched out
她发现可怜的动物躺在那里
and she was sure she had killed him
她确信自己已经杀死了他
she threw herself upon him without any dread
她毫无畏惧地扑向他
his heart was still beating
他的心脏仍在跳动
she fetched some water from the canal
她从运河里取了一些水
and she poured the water on his head
她把水倒在他头上
the Beast opened his eyes and spoke to Beauty
野兽睁开眼睛,对美丽说话
"You forgot your promise"
"你忘了你的承诺"
"I was so heartbroken to have lost you"
"失去你让我很伤心"
"I resolved to starve myself"
"我决定饿死自己"
"but I have the happiness of seeing you once more"
"但我很高兴再次见到你"
"so I have the pleasure of dying satisfied"
"所以我很开心能心满意足地死去"
"No, dear Beast," said Beauty, "you must not die"
"不,亲爱的野兽," 美女说, "你不能死。"
"Live to be my husband"
"活着做我的丈夫"
"from this moment I give you my hand"

"从这一刻起,我将我的手交给你"
"and I swear to be none but yours"
"我发誓我只属于你"
"Alas! I thought I had only a friendship for you"
"唉!我以为我对你只有友谊。"
"but the grief I now feel convinces me;"
"但我现在感受到的悲伤让我相信了这一点;"
"I cannot live without you"
"我不能没有你"
Beauty scarce had said these words when she saw a light
美女刚说完这些话,就看见一道光
the palace sparkled with light
宫殿里灯火辉煌
fireworks lit up the sky
烟花照亮了天空
and the air filled with music
空气中充满着音乐
everything gave notice of some great event
一切都预示着某件大事
but nothing could hold her attention
但没有什么能吸引她的注意力
she turned to her dear Beast
她转向她亲爱的野兽
the Beast for whom she trembled with fear
她害怕的野兽
but her surprise was great at what she saw!
但她所看到的景象让她更加惊讶!
the Beast had disappeared
野兽消失了
instead she saw the loveliest prince
她看到的却是最可爱的王子
she had put an end to the spell
她已经结束了咒语
a spell under which he resembled a Beast

咒语使他变得像野兽一样
this prince was worthy of all her attention
这位王子值得她全心全意关注
but she could not help but ask where the Beast was
但她忍不住问那只野兽在哪里
"You see him at your feet," said the prince
王子说："你看他就在你的脚下。"
"A wicked fairy had condemned me"
"一个邪恶的仙女判了我死刑"
"I was to remain in that shape until a beautiful princess agreed to marry me"
"我将保持这个样子，直到一位美丽的公主同意嫁给我"
"the fairy hid my understanding"
"仙女隐藏了我的理解"
"you were the only one generous enough to be charmed by the goodness of my temper"
"你是唯一一个如此慷慨的人，被我的善良脾气所吸引"
Beauty was happily surprised
美女惊喜不已
and she gave the charming prince her hand
她向迷人的王子伸出了手
they went together into the castle
他们一起进了城堡
and Beauty was overjoyed to find her father in the castle
美女在城堡里找到父亲，欣喜若狂
and her whole family were there too
她的家人也在场
even the beautiful lady that appeared in her dream was there
就连梦中出现的那位美人也在场
"Beauty," said the lady from the dream
"美女，"梦中的女士说
"come and receive your reward"

"来领取你的奖励"

"you have preferred virtue over wit or looks"
"你更看重美德，而不是智慧或外表"

"and you deserve someone in whom these qualities are united"
"你值得拥有这些品质的人"

"you are going to be a great queen"
"你将会成为一位伟大的女王"

"I hope the throne will not lessen your virtue"
"我希望王位不会贬低你的美德"

then the fairy turned to the two sisters
然后仙女转向两个姐妹

"I have seen inside your hearts"
"我看透了你们的内心"

"and I know all the malice your hearts contain"
"我知道你们心中充满的恶意"

"you two will become statues"
"你们两个会变成雕像的"

"but you will keep your minds"
"但你们要保持头脑清醒"

"you shall stand at the gates of your sister's palace"
"你应该站在你姐姐的宫殿门口"

"your sister's happiness shall be your punishment"
"你妹妹的幸福就是你的惩罚"

"you won't be able to return to your former states"
"你将无法回到以前的状态"

"unless, you both admit your faults"
"除非你们双方都承认自己的错误"

"but I am foresee that you will always remain statues"
"但我预见到你们将永远是雕像"

"pride, anger, gluttony, and idleness are sometimes conquered"
"骄傲、愤怒、暴食和懒惰有时会被征服"

"but the conversion of envious and malicious minds are

miracles"
"但嫉妒和恶意的心灵的转变是奇迹"
immediately the fairy gave a stroke with her wand
仙女立刻挥动魔杖
and in a moment all that were in the hall were transported
一瞬间,大厅里的所有人都被迷住了
they had gone into the prince's dominions
他们进入了王子的领地
the prince's subjects received him with joy
王子的臣民们热烈欢迎他
the priest married Beauty and the Beast
牧师为美女和野兽举行了婚礼
and he lived with her many years
他和她一起生活了很多年
and their happiness was complete
他们非常幸福
because their happiness was founded on virtue
因为他们的幸福建立在美德之上

The End
结束

www.ingramcontent.com/pod-product-compliance
Lightning Source LLC
Chambersburg PA
CBHW012011090526
44590CB00026B/3976